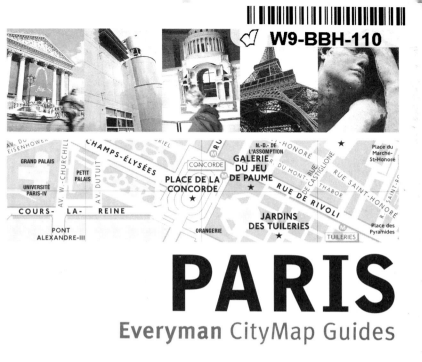

PARIS
Everyman CityMap Guides

HOW TO USE THIS GUIDE

The **Welcome to Paris!** fold-out provides valuable information, handy tips and useful addresses to help you make the most of your visit.

The area sections **A, B, C, D, E, F, G** and **H** have a double-page of addresses (restaurants - listed in ascending order of price - cafés, bars, music venues and stores) as well as a fold-out map for the relevant area with the essential places to see (indicated on the map by a star ★). These places are by no means all that Paris has to offer but to us they are unmissable.

The grid-referencing system (**A** B2) makes it easy for the reader to pinpoint addresses quickly on the map.

The **Transport and hotels in Paris** fold-out provides all the practical information you need to find your way around the city and a selection of the best hotels.

The **Thematic index** lists all the sites and addresses featured in this guide.

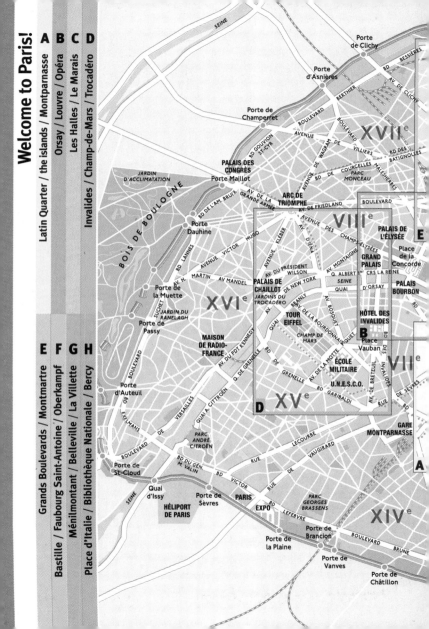

Welcome to Paris!

A Latin Quarter / the islands / Montparnasse
B Orsay / Louvre / Opéra
C Les Halles / Le Marais
D Invalides / Champ-de-Mars / Trocadéro

E Grands Boulevards / Montmartre
F Bastille / Faubourg Saint-Antoine / Oberkampf
G Ménilmontant / Belleville / La Villette
H Place d'Italie / Bibliothèque Nationale / Bercy

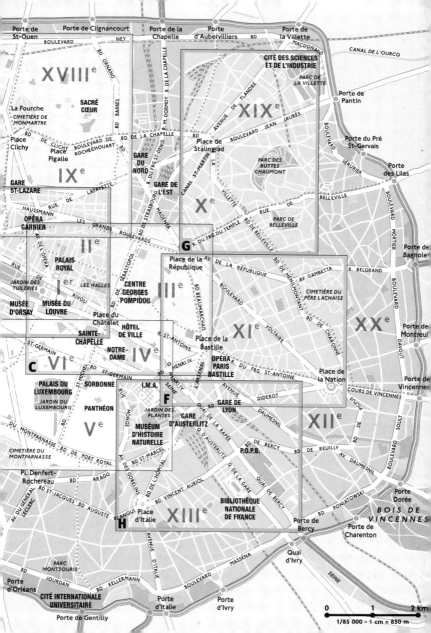

The Île de la Cité is the historic and geographic heart of Paris, filled with remnants of the old royal city. On the Rive Gauche (Left Bank) is St-Germain des-Prés with its post-war literary cafés, and the Quartier Latin with its art-house and experimental cinemas, universities and publishing houses. The Place de l'Odéon has held on to its former elegance, and the Rue St-André-des-Arts its medieval alleyways but the "Boul' Mich" (Bd St-Michel), joining onto the Luxembourg gardens, is now bereft of much of its former charm. It is worth making your way through the maze of streets around the Panthéon to the pretty Rue Mouffetard and its numerous little shops.

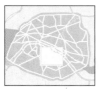

LA TAVERNE HENRY IV

KIOSQUE FLOTTANT

RESTAURANTS

Crêperie Josselin (A A3)
→ 67, rue du Montparnasse (14th)
Tel. 01 43 20 93 50
Tue-Fri noon–2.30pm,
6–11.30pm;
Sat-Sun noon–11pm.
No one should visit Montparnasse without stopping off to sample the famous *galettes bretonnes* (thick pancakes). Friendly atmosphere, typical Breton décor and superb crêpes. From 22F–57F per *galette*.

Taverne Henry IV (A D1)
→ 13, pl. du Pont-Neuf (1st) Tel. 01 43 54 27 90
Mon-Fri noon–8.30pm;
Sat noon–4pm. Closed Aug.
Robert Cointepas has manned the bar here for the past 40 years. More than 20 different types of wine available by the glass and delicious pork dishes from 30F.

Le Réminet (A E2)
→ 3, rue des Grands-Degrés (5th) Tel. 01 44 07 04 24
Closed Mon and Tue.
Chef Hugues Gourmay boldly marries different spices and flavors. Seasonal produce is cleverly integrated, with outstandingly delicious results. Reservations recommended in the evening. Set menu 110F, à la carte 210F.

Kiosque Flottant (A E2)
→ Port de Montebello (5th) Tel. 01 53 61 23 29
April–Sep: daily 10am–2pm
Sample a duck magret with raspberries in this splendid setting: a boat moored right at the foot of Notre-Dame.
À la carte 150F.

La Coupole (A C4)
→ 102, bd du Montparnasse (14th)
Tel. 01 43 20 14 20
Daily, continual service.
Once the meeting place of poets and writers in the 30s, today it still looks just the same, even after renovation. Art-Deco furnishings: painted pillars and chandeliers. Average cooking but good for people-watching. Set menu 189F, 138F after 10.30pm.

Bouillon Racine (A D2)
→ 3, rue Racine (6th)
Tel. 01 44 32 15 60
Daily 7.30am–midnight.
A credit to Belgium, this stunning sea-green Art-Nouveau setting offers thirty different beers. Fish *waterzooi* (soup), knuckle of lamb *confit* and exquisite coffee *liégeois* (coffee ice cream with whipped cream) served

DE LA MAIRIE | MARCHÉ AUX FLEURS | BOUQUINISTES

by the jug. La Gueuze et l'Écaille bar, adjacent to the restaurant, has seafood dishes and sells an impressive range of Belgian beers. Set menu 189F.

CAFÉS, TEAROOMS

Le Flore (A B1)
→ 172, bd St-Germain (6th)
Tel. 01 45 48 55 26
Daily 7am–1.30am.
Once the haunt of Left-Bank heroes such as Picasso, Hemingway, Camus and Sartre, this café still attracts the city's artists, intellectuals, and writers who've just been to see their editor in a nearby publishing house. The first floor tends to be a quieter place to sit. Pricey.

Café de la Mairie (A B2)
→ 8, pl. St-Sulpice (5th)
Tel. 01 43 26 67 82
Mon-Sat 7am–2am.
Opposite the church of St-Sulpice, this popular café has become the hang-out for literature lovers. The ashes of Nina Berberova were scattered just in front under the plane tree. Readings on Tue evenings except in summer. Pleasant terrace.

Charlotte de l'Île (A F2)
→ 24, rue Saint-Louis-en-

l'Île (4th) Tel. 01 43 54 25 83
Thu–Sun noon–8pm.
Tiny store with an enchanting décor where you can sample 36 blends of tea, divine hot chocolate and delicious fresh pastries.

La Viennoiserie (A C2)
→ 8, rue de l'École-de-Médecine (6th)
Tel. 01 43 26 60 48
Mon-Fri 9am–7pm.
Tiny patisserie-cum-tea room where a mixed crowd of regulars and students come on a daily basis for the delicious Jewish cakes, pastries, the enormous ice-cream floats and Viennese chocolates. Savory tarts and salads at lunchtime. Set menu 36F.

BARS, CINEMAS, MUSIC VENUES

La Villa (A C1)
→ 29, rue Jacob (6th)
Tel. 01 43 26 60 00
Mon-Sat 6pm–2am.
In the magnificent vaulted cellar of the modern hotel Villa St-Germain this has become since its opening in 1991 one of the city's leading jazz clubs. Top-quality music and performers.

Caveau de la Huchette (A D1)
→ 5, rue de la Huchette

(5th) Tel. 01 43 26 65 05
Daily from 9pm.
This medieval cellar-club has attracted rock 'n' roll fans for generations. Jazz and honky tonk piano at weekends.

Polly Magoo (A D2)
→ 11, rue Saint-Jacques (5th) Tel. 01 40 29 02 18
Daily noon–6am.
Discreet little bar with nicotine-stained posters, enticing nightowls in for a last drink.

Le Champo (A D2)
→ 51, rue des Écoles (5th)
Tel. 01 43 54 51 60
The most famous arthouse and independent cinema in the area.

Le P'tit Journal (A C3)
→ 71, bd St-Michel (5th)
Tel. 01 43 26 28 59
Mon-Sat 9am–2pm.
Atmosphere of 1950s St-Germain-des-Prés in this top-quality jazz venue with the sounds of Bolling, Zanini, Luter and Bailey.

SHOPPING

Berthillon (A F2)
→ 31, rue St-Louis-en-l'Île (4th) Tel. 01 43 54 31 61
Wed-Sun 10am–8pm.
Closed July-Aug.
Raspberry, mirabelle plum, honey, fig, nougat... This world-famous

ice-cream parlor boasts some 70 different flavors.
Marché aux Fleurs (A D1)
→ pl. Louis-Lépine (4th)
Daily 8am–7pm.
Flower market on the Île de la Cité: a tiny jungle right next to the Seine. Bird market on Sun.

Bouquinistes (A C1-E2)
→ Thu-Sun.
Since the 19th century this leafy row of second-hand book stalls has stood on the banks of the Seine: forgotten novels, anthologies of erotica, old maps and pre-war newspapers.

Le Bon Marché (A A2)
→ 24, rue de Sèvres (7th)
Tel. 01 44 39 80 00
Mon-Fri 9.30am–7pm;
Thu 9.30am–9pm;
Sat 9.30am–8pm.
Has become the most chic department store, complete with beauty treatment spa and high-quality delicatessen.

Christian Tortu (A C2)
→ Carrefour de l'Odéon (6th) Tel. 01 43 26 02 56
Mon-Sat 9am–8pm;
Sun 11am–7pm.
The shop window of this 'artist' (you wouldn't dare call him a florist) gives you some idea of what the Garden of Eden must have been like.

Orsay / Louvre / Opéra

The proximity of the Louvre Museum has made this district a firm favorite with tourists, giving the souvenir stores the chance to invade the arcades along the Rue de Rivoli. Nevertheless, the area has lost none of its grandeur. La Madeleine boasts a number of designer tableware stores and luxurious delis; top stylists' outlets and fashion designers line Rue Saint-Honoré and the arcades of Place Vendôme shelter the Ritz Hotel and the most famous jewelry stores. To escape the uproar of the streets head for the peaceful gardens of the Palais-Royal or the Tuileries.

IL CORTILE L'ENTRACTE

RESTAURANTS

Café Véry (**B** C3)
→ *Jardins des Tuileries (1st)*
Tel. 01 47 03 94 84
Daily noon–midnight.
A great place to enjoy the tranquility of the Tuileries gardens and sample a dish of chicken with morels or almond and cinnamon. Allow 70F for a full meal.

Il Cortile (**B** C2)
→ *37, rue Cambon (1st)*
Tel. 01 44 58 45 67
Mon-Fri noon–2.30pm,
7.30–10.30pm.
One of the best Italian restaurants in Paris, created by Alain Ducasse. Seasonal specialties: cuttlefish-ink cannelloni, risotto with asparagus, white Piedmont truffles... Lovely patio which is open in summer.
À la carte 300F.

Higuma (**B** E2)
→ *32 bis, rue St-Anne (1st)*
Tel. 01 47 03 38 59
Daily 11.30am–10pm.
Formica tables, cooks positioned in front of smoking woks ... ramen (flat noodles) and other Japanese specialties are served in this huge restaurant which attracts a clientele ranging from business people in a hurry to young *manga*-magazine readers. Set menus 35F, 63F and 70F.

Le Rouge Vif (**B** C4)
→ *48, rue de Verneuil (7th)*
Tel. 01 42 86 81 87
Mon-Fri noon–2.15pm,
8–10.45pm; Sat 8–10.45pm.
Excellent food bought fresh from the markets, obliging service, a cozy place. Set lunch menu 95F, dinner 180F–220F.

Le Grand Véfour (**B** E2)
→ *17, rue de Beaujolais (1st)*
Tel. 01 42 96 56 27
Mon-Fri 12.30–2.15pm,
7.30–10.15pm.
One of the oldest and most beautiful restaurants in Paris, situated under the arcades of the Palais-Royal. Fabulous, listed interior decor; comfortable, plush banquettes. Guy Martin, from Savoy, creates simple dishes which make the most of the quality of his produce. Remarkable wine list. Reservation advised. Set lunch menu 350F. À la carte 700F.

TEAROOMS

Angelina (**B** C3)
→ *226, rue de Rivoli (1st)*
Tel. 01 42 60 82 00
Daily 9am–7pm.
Opened in 1903 under the arcades in Rue de Rivoli,

FLANN O' BRIEN'S   COLETTE   DIDIER LUDOT

this English tearoom serves some of the best hot chocolate in Paris (36F), along with excellent desserts. Chocolates and pastries to go.

CAFÉS, BARS, MUSIC VENUES

Café Marly (B E3)
➔ *Palais du Louvre 93, rue de Rivoli (1st) Tel. 01 49 26 06 60 Daily 8am–2pm.*
An exceptional setting to stop for a drink and view I.M. Pei's pyramid and the French sculpture rooms of the Louvre museum. Pleasant service. Coffee 19F, draught beer 32F, lunch menu 250F.

L'Entracte (B E3)
➔ *47, rue de Montpensier (1st) Tel. 01 42 97 57 76 Mon-Fri 10am–2am; Sat-Sun noon–2am.*
This café has been around for centuries. Actors and audience alike from the Comédie-Française and the Théâtre du Palais-Royal come here for pre- or post-show drinks. Fresh, homemade food. Coffee 12F, draught beer 18F after 7.30pm.

Flann O' Brien's (B F3)
➔ *6, rue Bailleul (1st) Tel. 01 42 60 13 58 Daily 4pm–2am.*

Excellent Irish pub serving the smoothest Guinness in town (a pint: 39F). Darts board upstairs and excellent live music most nights.

Opéra Garnier (B D1)
➔ *Palais Garnier 8, rue Scribe (8th) Tel. 01 47 42 07 02*
Impressive neo-Renaissance and Baroque building dating from 1858. The auditorium ceiling was repainted by Chagall in 1964. Ballet, dance and opera performances. The library, museum, Grand Staircase and Foyer are open to the public.

SHOPPING

Samaritaine (B F4)
➔ *19, rue de la Monnaie (1st) Tel. 01 40 41 20 20 Mon-Sat 9.30am–7pm (until 10pm Thu).*
Department store situated right next to the Seine. You can buy anything you could possibly need here. Magnificent view of Paris from the roof-terrace.

Anna Joliet (B E2)
➔ *9, rue de Beaujolais (1st) Tel. 01 49 27 98 60 Mon-Sat 10am–7pm.*
Music boxes that will take you back to your child-hood. Over 60 different

tunes can be heard escaping from this little store hidden away beneath the arcades of the Palais-Royal. Expect to pay around 200F.

Sennelier (B D4)
➔ *3, quai Voltaire (7th) Tel. 01 42 60 72 15 Mon 2–7.30pm; Tue-Sat 9.30am–2pm.*
Walking into this three-story store is like opening an old paint box. Since 1887 Sennelier has supplied artists with papers, paints, pastels or lapis lazuli in powder form (at 2,000F for 10 gms) ... all with the Sennelier stamp.

Fauchon (B C2)
➔ *24, pl. de la Madeleine (8th) Tel. 01 47 42 60 11 Mon–Sat 9.30am–7pm (tearoom 8am–7pm).*
The most famous delicatessen in Paris: preserves, pastries, cold meats, wine, tea. An incredible range of fine and expensive goods.

Shiseido (B E3)
➔ *142, galerie de Valois (1st) Tel. 01 49 27 09 09 Mon-Sat 10am–7pm.*
Under the arcades of the Palais-Royal, a treasure trove of exotic perfumes created by Serge Lutens for Shiseido. Some scents on sale here are exclusive to this store.

Colette (B D3)
➔ *213, rue Saint-Honoré (1st) Tel. 01 55 35 33 90 Mon-Sat 10.30am–7.30pm.*
If it is tomorrow's fashion in clothes, art, cosmetics, jewelry, etc... Colette will have it before anybody else, and sell it ... at a price. There is a mineral water bar – the most exclusive of course – a dining room in the basement and a designers' exhibition on the 1st floor. Worth a visit, just for fun.

Didier Ludot (B E3)
➔ *24, galerie Montpensier (1st) Tel. 01 42 96 06 56 Mon-Sat 10.30am–7pm.*
Second-hand clothes, footwear, bags and cases whether by Chanel, Hermès, Balenciaga, Courrèges... Didier Ludot is a genuine collector of the best designs by the biggest names.

Le Louvre des Antiquaires (B E3)
➔ *2, pl. du Palais-Royal (1st) Tel. 01 42 97 27 00 Tue-Sun 11am–7pm. Closed Aug.*
Two hundred and fifty antiques dealers under the roof of a former department store. Spread over three floors are Louis XV furniture, china, gold, jewelry ...

The area around the Halles has been the focus of major building projects since the 1960s and makes up the heart of modern Paris. The Baltard houses, the churches of St-Eustache and of Beaubourg (the village) have all gone. The largest pedestrianized area in Europe stretches between Rue Montorgueil and the gates of St-Martin and St-Denis. Pop into the Georges-Pompidou center or explore the old quartier of Le Marais, a listed area since 1962. Here the 17th-century townhouses and narrow winding streets contain a mixture of Jewish stores, quirky, trendy boutiques, antique dealers and gay bars.

TRUMILOU · L'ESCARGOT DE MONTORGUEIL

RESTAURANTS

Minh Chau (**C** D3)
→ 10, rue de la Verrerie (4th) Tel. 01 42 71 13 30
Daily 9am–midnight.
Tiny Vietnamese restaurant where you can drop in for a quick bite to eat: peppered pork or shrimp curry (20–25F) accompanied by a cup of tea (3F). Very friendly.
Chez Marianne (**C** E3)
→ 2, rue des Hospitalières-Saint-Gervais (4th)
Tel. 01 42 72 18 86 Daily.
Charming delicatessen where you can sample Jewish and Eastern European fare. An abundance of meze: fallafel, kefta, tabouleh, stuffed vine leaves... You can also take out. Good choice for vegetarians. Book in advance. À la carte 55–75F.
Jo Goldenberg (**C** E3)
→ 7, rue des Rosiers (4th)
Tel. 01 48 87 20 16
Daily 9am–midnight.
A shrine to Ashkenazi cooking: borscht, stuffed carp, chopped liver and onions, chicken soup. Inviting atmosphere and music. Daily special 80F.
Trumilou (**C** B2)
→ 84, quai de l'Hôtel-de-Ville (4th) Tel. 01 42 77 63 98
Daily noon–3pm, 7–11pm.

Small dishes to suit all budgets. Traditional and simple cuisine, just like home-cooking. Set menus 80F, 98F.
Chez Omar (**C** E2)
→ 47, rue de Bretagne (3rd) Tel. 01 42 72 36 26
Closed Sun lunch.
Traditional brasserie and the best couscous in Paris, cooked by Omar himself. À la carte 120F.
La Mule du Pape (**C** F3)
→ 8, rue du Pas de la Mule (3rd) Tel. 01 42 74 55 80
Mon–Fri 11am–6pm, 7–11pm
Sat 11am–11pm;
Sun 11am–7pm.
A few yards away from the Place des Vosges, this is a small, homely, cozy restaurant. Provençale specialties; home-made desserts. Salad with foie gras and one glass of wine 100F. À la carte 150F. Wines by the glass. It is advisable to book.
L'Escargot de Montorgueil (**C** C2)
→ 38, rue Montorgueil (1st) Tel. 01 42 36 83 51
Daily noon–3pm, 7–11pm.
An excellent place to taste delicious Burgundy snails in an 1870s setting.

TEAROOMS

L'Ébouillanté (**C** D3)
→ 6, rue des Barres (4th)

UILLANTÉ   LE LATINA   VILLAGE SAINT-PAUL

Tel. 01 42 71 09 69
Tue-Sun noon–10pm (9pm
in winter).
In a pedestrianized street
opposite the church of
St-Gervais-St-Protais.
Mellow jazz is played in
the book-lined interior,
decorated in blue. The
terrace is perfect for afternoon tea. Set menu 75F.

Marais Plus (C E3)
→ 20, rue des Francs-
Bourgeois (3rd)
Tel. 01 48 87 01 40
Daily 10am–7.30pm.
Store and tearoom selling
fascinating and unusual
toys, large and small.
Exquisite savory and
sweet tarts (eat in or take
out).

Le Loir dans la Théière
(C E3)
→ 3, rue des Rosiers (6th)
Tel. 01 42 72 90 61
Mon-Fri 11.30am–7pm;
Sat-Sun 10am–7pm.
Sink into the comfortable
old leather armchairs and
enjoy a salad or delicious
pastry. Excellent service.
Savory tarts 48F, salads
45F.

CAFÉS, BARS, THEATERS, MUSIC VENUES

Web Bar (C E2)
→ 32, rue de Picardie (3rd)
Tel. 01 42 72 66 55

Daily 11.30am–2am.
A heaven for cyberfans,
this old silversmith work
shop, converted into an
Internet café, has plenty
more to offer: poetry
nights, debates, chess,
concerts, art exhibitions...

Café Beaubourg (C D3)
→ 43, rue St-Merri (4th)
Tel. 01 48 87 63 96
Daily 8am–1am.
Opposite the Pompidou
center, this is the most
chic café in the area, with
an extraordinary design
by architect Christian de
Portzamparc.
À la carte 175F.

Duc des Lombards
(C C3)
→ 42, rue des Lombards
(1st) Tel. 01 42 33 22 88
Tue-Sat from 9pm;
Sun-Mon: times vary
depending on the program.
The poster-covered walls
trace the history of jazz.
Innovative line-up with a
bias toward modern
European jazz. Entrance
100F; drinks 28F.

Le Petit Opportun (C C3)
→ 15, rue des Lavandières-
Sainte-Opportune (1st)
Tel. 01 42 36 01 36
Tue–Sat from 10.30pm.
Small club that welcomes
musicians from the
French jazz scene, both
newcomers and old
timers alike: swing,

bebop, New Orleans jazz.
Entrance 50–80F.

Café de la Gare (C D3)
→ 41, rue du Temple (4th)
Tel. 01 42 78 52 51
Daily 8pm and 10pm.
The nicest of the café-
théâtres, this venue has
hosted comics, popular
theater and children's
shows (at 3pm) for 30
years. Entrance 100F.

Le Latina (C D3)
→ 20, rue du Temple (4th)
Tel. 01 42 78 47 86
Since 1913 Le Latina
has screened the best
of Italian, Spanish,
Portuguese and Latin-
American films. On the
first floor is a bar and
dance floor complete with
strutting tango dancers.

Amnesia (C E3)
→ 42, rue Vieille-du-Temple
(4th) Tel. 01 42 72 16 94
Daily 9.30am–2am.
Ivy-fronted gay bar.
A colorful clientele and
1980s music in the
basement. Salad and
daily specials 45F.

SHOPPING

Forum des Halles (C C2)
→ Rues Berger and
Rambuteau (1st) Mon-Sat.
Several hundred stores
(one of which is FNAC),
movie theater and
swimming pool.

Mariage Frères (C D3)
→ 30, rue du Bourg-Tibourg
(4th) Tel. 01 42 72 28 11
Daily 10.30am–7.30pm
(store), noon–7pm (rest).
Magnificent colonial-style
store packed with huge
round pots containing
350 varieties of tea from
all over the world.
Sample in house or take
out. Brunch on Sun from
noon–6.30pm.
À la carte 80–150F.

BHV (C D3)
→ 52, rue de Rivoli (4th)
Tel. 01 42 77 44 79
Mon–Sat 9.30am–7pm
The place for DIY
enthusiasts. The Bazar
de l'Hôtel-de-Ville, right
in the heart of Paris, also
sells high fashion, toys
perfume, books and
electric appliances.

Village Saint-Paul
(C E4)
→ Rues Charlemagne and
Saint-Paul (4th) Thu-Mon.
An entire colony of little
antique stores situated
between Rue Saint-Paul
and Rue Charlemagne
along quiet passageways
and courtyards.

Finkelstajn (C E3)
→ 27, rue des Rosiers (4th)
Tel. 01 42 72 78 91
Wed-Mon 10am–7pm.
The best Jewish deli in
Paris: Russian and central
European specialties.

From La Concorde, the Champs-Élysées is an unforgettable sight. The famous throughfare stretches majestically to the Arc de Triomphe. Restaurants, cafés, chic night-clubs and even expensive car show-rooms draw a colorful crowd day and night. Avenue Montaigne, the epitome of luxury and home to Chanel, Christian Dior, Louis Vuitton, Nina Ricci and Christian Lacroix, the best couturiers and designers, descends toward the Seine. Les Invalides and the Champ-de-Mars stretch along the opposite bank, lined with lovely townhouses and offering impressive views of the Eiffel Tower.

APOLLON | CAFÉ THOUMIEUX

RESTAURANTS

Apollon (D C3)
➔ 24, rue Jean-Nicot (7th)
Tel. 01 45 55 68 47
Last orders 11pm; closed Sun.
A tiny restaurant full of Mediterranean color. Cheese from Cyprus, basil, feta and tomato salads, *souvlakis* (kebabs), ground-rice cake with lemon zest. Lunch menu 85F .

L'Ami-Jean (D C3)
➔ 27, rue Malar (7th)
Tel. 01 47 05 86 89
Closed Sun.
The photos hanging on the walls tell you that you have entered Basque country. Friendly service with an eclectic clientele. The south-west French cuisine includes: magret of duck, Spanish omelette, and Basque gâteau. Daily specials 74–92F; à la carte 180F; set menu 99F.

Noura (D B2)
➔ 21–27, ave. Marceau (16th) Tel. 01 47 23 02 20
Daily until midnight.
One of the best Lebanese restaurants in Paris. Plates of *meze* at 68F, *chawarma* chicken-tabouleh 84F and pastries 24F. Excellent wine list, all available by the glass.

Le Bistrot de Marius Rive Gauche (D D4)
➔ 74, bd de la Tour-Maubourg (7th)
Tel. 01 47 53 80 86
Daily noon–2.30pm, 7–10.30pm.
This is one of the best fish restaurants in Paris: very fresh produce and simple, delicious dishes. Even better: it is open on Sun. Entrées 48F, main course up to 145F, desserts c.38F.

Tampopo (D A2)
➔ 66, rue Lauriston (16th)
Tel. 01 47 27 74 52
Closed Sat lunch and Sun.
Nothing like the hectic Japanese restaurants on Rue Ste-Anne. Here you remove your shoes at the door and step into an atmosphere of zen calm and serenity; ancient traditions of Japanese cooking. Set menus 90F and 120F at lunchtime, 150F dinner.

La Fermette Marbeuf 1900 (D C2)
➔ 5, rue Marbeuf (8th)
Tel. 01 53 23 08 00
Daily noon–3pm, 7pm–midnight.
Gilbert Isaac's excellent kitchen serves traditional cooking in a stunning Art-Nouveau décor. Pleasant terrace and a truly good wine list. Set menu 180F.

CHRISTIAN LACROIX

CHANEL

FAGUAIS

La Maison de l'Alsace (**D** C1)

→ 39, ave. des
Champs-Élysées (8th)
Tel. 01 53 93 97 00
Daily 24 hours.
This large brasserie on Champs-Élysées never closes and serves some of the best Alsatian food in Paris. Saueurkraut, roasted suckling pig, incredibly fresh seafood platters. À la carte 250F.

TEAROOMS

Ladurée (**D** C1)

→ 75, ave. des Champs-Élysées (8th)
Tel. 01 40 75 08 75
Daily 7.30am–1am.
Thirty flavors of macaroons including coffee, chocolate, vanilla, rose petal and Guérande caramel. All served against a backdrop of stucco, gilt and marble. Genteel service.
The other Ladurée is at 16, rue Royale (8th).
18F large macaroon, 7.50F small.

CAFÉS, BARS, MUSIC VENUES

Café du Musée Rodin (**D** D4)

→ 77, rue de Varenne (7th)
Tel. 01 45 50 42 34 Tue–
Sun 10am–6pm (4.30pm in winter).
Enjoy a pleasant drink or snack in the tranquil setting of the Rodin Museum statue garden. Entrance fee to the garden 5F.

Café Thoumieux (**D** C3)

→ 4, rue de la Comète (7th) Tel. 01 45 51 50 40
Mon-Fri noon–2am;
Sat 7pm–2am.
Red velvet décor enjoyed by a young sophisticated clientele. Excellent cocktails 50F, tapas 60F and a huge screen showing sports events.

Master's Bar (**D** C4)

→ 64, ave. Bosquet (7th)
Tel. 01 45 51 08 99
Daily 9am–2am.
Thierry Delamare's famous cocktails. Happy hour during the week from 5–7pm. Cocktails 48–58F.

Le Doobie's (**D** C2)

→ 2, rue Robert-Estienne (8th) Tel. 01 53 76 10 76
Mon-Sat 6pm–2am;
Sun noon–2am.
A favorite with the fashion set. Cozy and intimate. Cocktails 60F.

Au Dernier Métro (**D** A5)

→ 70, bd de Grenelle (15th)
Tel. 01 45 75 01 23
Daily 6am–2am.
A bar in a colorful

quartier where you can choose between 10 different draught beers alongside friends and locals. Lively atmosphere, especially on soccer match nights! Excellent south-west French cuisine. Main course 58–90F.

Le Queen (**D** C1)

→ 102, ave. des
Champs-Élysées (8th)
Tel. 01 53 89 08 90
Daily midnight–dawn.
This major club is one of the best Parisian gay bars. Erotic dancing for men only on Thursday and Saturday.
Themed nights: 'Disco' (Mon), 'Private' (Tue), 'Secret' (Wed), 'French variety' (Thu), 'House' (Fri-Sat) and '1980-90s' (Sun).

Théâtre des Champs-Élysées (**D** C2)

→ 15, ave. Montaigne (8th)
Tel. 01 49 52 50 50
Mon-Sat. Closed July–Aug.
Opera, lyric opera, chamber music (on Sundays the Orchestre National of France) and contemporary dance under the direction of Dominique Meyer. Tickets 40–450F.
The theater's rooftop restaurant, Maison Blanche '15 Montaigne' offers gastronomic food

and a breathtaking view of Paris.

SHOPPING

La Maison du Chocolat (**D** C1)

→ 56, rue Pierre-Charron (8th) Tel. 01 47 23 38 25
Mon-Sat 10am–7.30pm.
Chocolate in all possible forms: macaroons, chocolate bars, candies, drinks, pastries ... Heaven on earth for chocoholics.

Faguais (**D** C2)

→ 30, rue de La Trémoille (8th) Tel. 01 47 20 80 91
Mon-Sat 9.30am–7pm.
Traditional-style grocery store. More than 2,000 kinds of produce made by traditional methods: Montélimar nougat, Agen prunes, Calissons d'Aix (almond paste sweets), teas, preserves and 50 rare coffee blends.

Virgin Mega store (**D** C1)

→ 52, ave. des
Champs-Élysées (8th)
Tel. 49 53 50 00
Mon-Sat 10am–midnight,
Sun and public holidays noon–midnight.
In a lovely 1930s building: books, music, videos and on the top floor the Virgin Café, where you can grab a bite to eat or just stop for a drink. Daily specials 50–60F, à la carte 150F.

The Sacré-Cœur, perched at the top of La Butte, attracts tourists from all over the world. The artists, cabarets and balls of the Belle Époque may be long gone but the old charm of Montmartre lives on in the steep streets, stairways and pretty, ivy-covered houses. As evening falls the concert halls on the boulevards fill up and the sex scene in Pigalle begins to come to life. Two minutes away the Nouvelle Athène entices visitors with the romantic charm of its quiet little streets and Directoire-style architecture – an oasis in the midst of the bustle of the big boulevards.

BOUILLON CHARTIER   L'ÉTÉ EN PENTE DOUCE

RESTAURANTS

Le Zouave Gobichon (E B3)
→ 8, rue Durantin (18th)
Tel. 01 46 06 25 75
Closed Sun lunch and Mon.
Small, cozy dining room serving good quality, varied French cuisine. Zouave often invites local artists to exhibit their works here. Vegetarian special 69F.

L'Été en Pente Douce (E B2)
→ 23, rue Muller (18th)
Tel. 01 42 64 02 67. Daily.
Restaurant and tearoom with a large terrace. Salads 48–56F, traditional dishes 72–95F. Seasonal and vegetarian menus.

Bouillon Chartier (E C6)
→ 7, rue du Faubourg-Montmartre (9th)
Tel. 01 47 70 86 29. Daily 11.30am–3pm, 6–10pm.
Superb Belle Époque canteen serving cheap, straightforward cooking in the midst of a pleasant hubbub. Set menu 78F.

Le Mono (E B3)
→ 40, rue Véron (18th)
Tel. 01 46 06 99 20
Mon-Tue and Thu-Sun 7–11.30pm (lunch by reservation).
Typical décor, music and food from Togo. Specialties include: gbekui (smoked fish in spinach sauce), chicken djenkoumé (half wheat, half corn-meal pastry) and braised fish in moyo (mild spices). À la carte 100F.

Per Bacco (E D3)
→ 10, rue Lambert (18th)
Tel. 01 42 52 22 40
Mon-Fri noon–2.30pm, 8–10.30pm; Sat 8–10.30pm.
The Naples-born chef of this restaurant has his produce sent direct from Italy. Authentic cuisine in an unpretentious setting. Attentive service. À la carte 200F.

Beauvilliers (E C2)
→ 52, rue Lamarck (18th)
Tel. 01 42 54 54 42.
Closed Sun and Mon lunch.
The most prestigious restaurant on la Butte, run by maître d' Édouard Carlier. Elegantly imaginative gastronomy: grilled red mullet in fine escabèche (marinaded and served cold), artichoke hearts stuffed with crab. Set menu 185F lunch, 400F dinner (including wine).

BARS, CLUBS, CABARET

Le Sancerre (E B3)
→ 35, rue des Abbesses (18th) Tel. 01 42 58 08 20
This trendy café-bar is

N-ROUGE   PRINTEMPS   ART'S FACTORY

located in the heart of the Abbesses district. At its best in the late afternoon and evening when the terrace is inundated with locals.

La Fourmi (**E** C5)
→ 74, rue des Martyrs (18th) Tel. 01 42 64 70 35
Daily 8am–2am.
Café situated at the crossroads of the trendy section of Pigalle, and near La Cigale, the famous concert hall (La cigale et la fourmi is one of La Fontaine's Fables). Good crowd and a fashionable place to be seen. Ideal for breakfast or a snack (salads, sandwiches and daily specials).

Élysée-Montmartre (**E** C4)
→ 72, bd Rochechouart (18th) Tel. 01 55 07 06 00
Originally a ballroom (1807) this has become a leading light on the Paris dance scene. Fans of alternative rock or world music sway under the 1900s molding. Live band and DJ every other Sat.

Divan du Monde (**E** C5)
→ 75, rue des Martyrs (18th) Tel. 01 44 92 77 66
World music (African, Brazilian, Caribbean, Oriental) and also themed evenings, films

and dance in this former Belle Époque cabaret venue.

Rex Club (**E** D6)
→ 5, bd Poissonnière (2nd) Tel. 01 42 36 10 96
Wed-Sat 11am–dawn.
Parisian home of electronic music presided over by the best DJs of the moment.

Moulin-Rouge (**E** B4)
→ 82, bd de Clichy (18th) Tel. 01 53 09 82 82
Daily 7pm (dinner); 9pm, 10pm, (shows).
A Paris institution! Reservation essential.

Max Linder (**E** C6)
→ 24, bd Poissonnière (9th) Tel. 01 48 24 00 47
1930s Art-Deco cinema. Large screen, state-of-the-art sound system and a bar on the ground floor.

SHOPPING

Art's Factory (**E** C4)
→ 48, rue d'Orsel (18th) Tel. 01 53 28 13 50
Tue-Sat 11am–7.30pm; Sun 2–7pm.
Dynamic art gallery exhibiting – and selling – contemporary works (paintings, sculpture, photos, objects etc.). Their mission is to promote 'Cheap Art', art which is within everyone's price range.

Patricia Louisor (**E** C4)
→ 16, rue Houdon (18th) Tel. 01 42 62 10 42
Daily noon–8pm.
Young stylist in the heart of the fashionable square delineated by Pigalle-Abbesses-Anvers. Fashion that is imaginative, original and also affordable.

Pain d'Épice (**E** C6)
→ 29 passage Jouffroy (2nd) Tel. 01 47 70 08 68
Mon 12.30–7pm; Tue-Sun 10am–7pm.
A most amazing toy store. Ancient dolls, accessories for children's parties, wooden mobiles, cots, trains, miniature soldiers and collectors' items.

Department stores (**E** A6)

Le Printemps
→ 64, bd Haussmann (9th) Mon-Sat 9.35am–7pm (until 10pm Thu).

Les Galeries Lafayette (**E** A6)
→ 40, bd Haussmann (9th) Mon-Sat 9.30am–6.45pm (until 9pm Thu).
The two best department stores on the Boulevard. Printemps boasts stucco, Belle Époque, Art Deco, and listed 19th-century glass. Top brand names, accessories and an astonishing range of services. Lafayette Gourmet, next door,

is a favorite with foodies and wine lovers. Grab a bite there (tastings every lunchtime) or take out.

Tati (**E** D4)
→ 4, bd Rochechouart (18th) Tel. 01 55 29 50 00
Mon–Sat 10am–7pm.
www.tati.fr
Open in 1948, this is the first of the Tati stores. 'The lowest prices' in town and guaranteed entertainment!

Marché St-Pierre (**E** C3)
→ 2, rue Charles-Nodier (18th) Tel. 01 46 06 92 25
Mon 1.30–6.30pm; Wed-Sat 10am–6.30pm.
Truly the best place to buy fabric, attracting sewing enthusiasts, designers and interior decorators. Over a 2,400-sq-yds area flannel, tweed, silk, linen, cotton, ticking, sequined and floral fabrics sold by the meter.

Puces de Saint-Ouen et Clignancourt (**E** C1)
→ Porte de Clignancourt (18th) Sat-Mon 9.30am–7pm
The oldest and largest of Parisian flea markets: 2,000 outlets, 9 miles to walk and 150,000 visitors each week! Bric-à-brac and specialist markets: Biron (antiques), Malik (fashion), Malassis (art), Serpette (second-hand goods) …

Place de la Bastille is where the capital's dedicated nightlife begins. Cafés, bars and restaurants line the surrounding streets: Rue du Faubourg-St-Antoine, Rue de la Roquette, Rue de Lappe and Rue de Charonne. But carry on further west along the Rue du Faubourg-St-Antoine and take a peek at the maze of courtyards and passageways. Cabinet-makers, for whom this area is renowned, now live alongside designers, architects, graphic designers and stylists. The Oberkampf area, north of Bastille, has now become the hippest, trendiest place to hang out in Paris, attracting nightowls on the prowl for new haunts.

LES AMOGNES

JACQUES MÉLAC

RESTAURANTS

Paris Main d'Or (F C3)
→ *133, rue du Faubourg-Saint-Antoine (11th)
Tel. 01 44 68 04 68
Mon-Sat noon–3pm, 8–11pm.*
Tasty rustic cooking from Corsica: vegetables stuffed with *broccio* cheese, roast goat with potatoes. Set lunch menu 69F, Corsican specialties à la carte.

L'Ébauchoir (F D4)
→ *45, rue de Cîteaux (12th)
Tel. 01 43 42 49 31
Mon-Sat noon–2.30pm, 8–11pm.*
A restaurant reflecting the local craft industry. Simple but good fare: lentil salad, beef *bourguignon*, crème caramel. 3-course lunch menu (incl. wine) 70F.

La Mère Lachaise (F E1)
→ *78, bd de Ménilmontant (20th) Tel. 01 47 97 61 60
Daily 8am–midnight.*
Subdued décor extending onto the large terrace. On the menu, mixed salads, pies and daily specials. À la carte 90F.

Le Square Trousseau (F C4)
→ *1, rue Antoine-Vollon (11th) Tel. 01 43 43 06 00
Daily noon–2.30pm, 8–11.30pm.*

This attractive bistro offers straightforward cooking, using the best market produce; it caters to a trendy, chic, local clientele. Excellent wine list. À la carte 200F.

Chez Paul (F C3)
→ *13, rue de Charonne (11th) Tel. 01 47 00 34 57
Daily noon–2.30pm, 7pm–midnight.*
An institution in the quartier, nestled behind the crumbling exterior of an old house in the Rue de Charonne. Seafood salad with *foie gras*, grilled peppered steak. À la carte 160F.

Les Amognes (F E4)
→ *243, rue du Faubourg-Saint-Antoine (11th)
Tel. 01 43 72 73 05
Mon 7.30–10.30pm;
Tue-Sat noon–2pm, 7.30–10.30pm (until 11pm Sat).*
Fresh marinated sardine tart, sautéed squid with garlic and vegetables, crêpe stuffed with eggplant and cardamon. Thierry Coué's kitchen presents seasonal cooking which is both affordable and of good quality. Set menu 180F.

Chardenoux (F D3)
→ *1, rue Jules Vallès (11th)
Mon-Fri noon–2pm, 8–10pm; Sat 8–10.30pm.*
Shiny moldings and a

LA BAGUE DE KENZA   VIADUC DES ARTS   BO PLASTIC

long counter... an old bistro that will take you back in time. Classic cuisine, complimented by inventive specialties (sweet and sour tarts with spiced *confit* of lamb). À la carte 250F.

Blue Elephant (F C3)
➔ *43, rue de la Roquette (11th) Tel. 01 47 00 42 00 Closed Sat lunch.*
A tropical paradise: teak wood paneling, luxuriant greenery, Thaï orchids, a fountain splashing gently in the background. Excellent Thai cuisine. À la carte 250F.

CAFÉS, BARS, OPERA

Jacques Mélac (F E3)
➔ *42, rue Léon-Frot (11th) Tel. 01 43 70 59 27 Mon 9am–5pm; Tue-Sat 9am–midnight.*
Vines trail over the front of Chez Mélac. Drinking water here is strongly discouraged! Wine, 20-25F a glass, is accompanied by plates of *charcuterie* from the Aveyron region (55F), cheese from Cantal or a hot dish.

Le Café du Passage (F C3)
➔ *12, rue de Charonne (11th) Tel. 01 49 29 97 64 Daily noon–2am.*

English décor. Snacks and excellent wines, whiskies and champagne.

L'Entrepôt (F C3)
➔ *14, rue de Charonne (11th) Tel. 01 48 06 57 04 Daily until 2am.*
Iron staircase, sofas, old photographs hanging on the walls and atmospheric music playing in the background. Cocktails: Happy Hour from 5 till 8.30pm.

Le Lèche-Vin (F B3)
➔ *13, rue Daval (11th) Tel. 01 43 55 98 91 Tue-Thu 6pm–1am (until 2am Fri-Sat).*
Religious souvenirs of all sorts – icons of the Virgin Mary, Christ and the saints – along with draught beer, loud music and a young clientele ... The décor even extends to the W.Cs!

Le Café Charbon (F C1)
➔ *109, rue Oberkampf (11th) Tel. 01 43 57 55 13 Daily until 2am.*
Industrial-style décor (gas lamps, zinc bar) and a very trendy clientele. À la carte 130F.

Les Couleurs (F C1)
➔ *117, rue Saint-Maur (11th) Tel. 01 43 57 95 61 Daily until 2am.*
The look here is resolutely grunge, with non-matching formica

tables and old nicotine-stained walls. Lemon punch all day.

Le Balajo (F C3)
➔ *9, rue de Lappe (11th) Tel. 01 47 00 07 87 Wed-Sun.*
Opened in 1936, the 'Bal à Jo' revives the tradition of the tea dance, with live accordion music every Thursday and Sunday. There are classes in Argentinian tango during the week as well as rock 'n' roll or salsa classes in the evening. Kitsch 1930s setting.

Opéra Bastille (F B3)
➔ *pl. de la Bastille (11th)* Tel. 08 36 69 78 68 for *information / reservations* Opera, lyric opera, classical ballet. Reserve several weeks in advance.

SHOPPING

La Bague de Kenza (F C1)
➔ *106, rue Saint-Maur (11th) Tel. 01 43 14 93 15 Daily 9.30am–9pm.*
The best Algerian pastries in Paris. Wide choice of breads and savory specialties.

Cooperativa Cisternino (F C1)
➔ *108, rue Saint-Maur (11th) Tel. 01 48 01 05 02 Mon-Sat 10am–1.30pm, 4-8pm; Sun 10am–1.30pm.*
Reasonably priced

cheeses *(mozzarella pecorino, parmesan)* and quality *charcuterie* from the Iberian Peninsula.

Viaduc des Arts (F C4)
➔ *ave. Daumesnil (12th)*
Ceramics, tapestry, sculpture, cabinetmaking, painting and much more: over 45 designers and highly skilled craftworkers occupy the vaults of this viaduct, renovated in 1990.

Galerie Gaultier (F C3)
➔ *30, rue du Faubourg-Saint-Antoine (11th) Tel. 01 44 68 84 84 Mon-Sat 11am–7.30pm.*
Clothes and accessories by Jean-Paul, the *enfant terrible* of the French fashion world.

Bo Plastic (F C3)
➔ *31, rue de Charonne (11th) Tel. 01 53 36 73 16 Mon-Sat 11am–8pm.*
Plastic creations, mostly from the 60s and 70s, for collectors or 60s design junkies. Exhibitions too.

FNAC Bastille (F B3)
➔ *4, pl. de la Bastille (12th) Tel. 01 43 42 04 04 Mon-Sat 10am–8pm (until 10pm Wed and Fri).*
Unlike the other branches of FNAC, here music takes pride of place. Specialist service. Ticket booth for concerts.

Along the canals, Paris past and Paris present stand side by side. A walk along the banks of the Canal St-Martin is full of old-fashioned charm. The Canal de l'Ourq, by contrast, continues as far as La Villette, where a thoroughly 21st-century park suddenly appears out of nowhere. Further south the Park des Buttes-Chaumont, reformed in 1864 to rehabilitate the surrounding slum area, has given birth to a respectable residential district. Below it are the working-class villages of Belleville and Ménilmontant, rich with the influence of immigrants from Asia and the Orient.

LE BARATIN

RESTAURANTS

Benesti (G C6)
→ *108, bd de Belleville (20ᵗʰ) Tel. 01 44 55 44 55 Tue-Sun.*
Wonderful Jewish Tunisian snacks: falafel sandwiches, *brik*, *choudchouka*, Tunisian salads, mint tea and pastries. A place where people eat lots and talk even more! An extra-ordinary taste of the Mediterranean. Dinner 50–70F.

Le Baratin (G C5)
→ *3, rue Jouye-Rouve (20ᵗʰ) Tel. 01 43 49 39 70 Tue-Sat noon–2.30pm, 8.30–11.30pm.*
Impressive wine list compiled by patron Olivier Camus (there are 200 different wines on the menu). Excellent cuisine based around seasonal availability. Friendly atmosphere, unpretentious setting. Lunch menu 73F.

La Boulangerie (G D6)
→ *15, rue des Panoyaux (20ᵗʰ) Tel. 01 43 58 45 45 Daily except Sat lunch.*
This restaurant at the front of a traditional bakery, opened its doors in May 1999. The décor is as delicious as the cooking: *effilochade* of

dried duck with cardamom and creamed lentils, salt beef followed by Ménilmontant tart for dessert. Set menu, lunch 68F, dinner 98F.

L'Heure Bleue (G D4)
→ *57, rue Arthur Rozier (19ᵗʰ) Tel 01 42 39 18 07 Mon-Fri noon–2.30pm, 7–10.45pm; Sat eve only 7–10.45pm*
Good traditional cuisine with a south west touch (duck *confit*, foie gras) but also a wide range of very good vegetarian dishes (vegetable ravioli, savoury tarts). Set menu 65F (lunchtime only); à la carte 120-150F.

L'Atlantide (G C3)
→ *7, ave. Laumière (19ᵗʰ) Tel. 01 42 45 09 81 Tue-Sun 7.30pm–midnight.*
Dine here and sample the best Berber specialties: couscous of fine semolina served with a choice of sauce or fresh steamed vegetables. The meat is succulent, particularly the *tajine* dishes (with dried fruits or vegetables). À la carte 150F.

La Cave Gourmande (G D4)
→ *10, rue du Gᵃˡ-Brunet (19ᵗʰ) Tel. 01 40 40 03 30 Mon-Fri noon–2pm, 7–10pm.*
Restaurant, delicatessen

PASCALOU   MARCHÉ DE BELLEVILLE   ÉPICERIE LE CAIRE

and wine merchant where fine food is always on offer. The choice is somewhat limited, but the menu changes daily. Set menu only, 170F.

Krung Thep (G C5)
→ *93, rue Julien-Lacroix (20th) Tel. 01 43 66 83 74 Daily 6pm–midnight.*
It's difficult to imagine that behind these smoked-glass windows lurks one of the the best Thai restaurants in Paris. Exotic setting, efficient service and, above all, delicious food with subtle and unusual combinations of flavors: sweet salad with banana flower, wrapped chicken, *pat thaï* (noodles sautéed with shrimp)... If the place is full, go straight to Lao Siam, *49, rue de Belleville,* instead.

CAFÉS, BARS, MUSIC VENUES

La Maroquinerie (G D6)
→ *23, rue Boyer (20th) Tel. 01 40 33 30 60 Closed Sun.*
This fashionable venue, with its ultra-modern décor used to be an old leather workshop, tucked away in a courtyard. Its concerts, exhibitions readings and debates

encourage meetings between local inhabitants and artists.
Daily specials 50–60F.
Lou Pascalou (G D6)
→ *14, rue des Panoyaux (20th) Tel. 01 46 36 78 10 Daily 9am–2pm.*
Understated, but cozy, a limited number of tables and a terrace, obliging waiters... A popular, no-nonsense place, like its regulars. Rock or world music concerts and, occasionally, theater evenings.

Le Soleil (G C6)
→ *136, bd de Ménilmontant (20th). Tel. 01 46 36 47 44 Daily until 2am.*
Four rows of tables on the terrace spill out onto the sidewalk, tempting passersby. Sip a mint tea, a *pastis,* or a draught beer. Attracts a friendly, mixed crowd.

Aux Folies (G C5)
→ *8, rue de Belleville (19th) Tel. 01 46 36 65 98 Daily 6am–midnight.*
The neon sign conjures up the old Belleville. Here, in the 1930s, a café-theater drew the biggest names, from Édith Piaf to Yves Montand. Amar, who has now taken over the venue, has kept the original

décor. An unpretentious place where you can have a drink at the bar, or on the terrace, and sit watching the world go by.

Cité de la Musique (G D2)
→ *Parc de La Villette 221, ave. Jean-Jaurès (19th) Tel. 01 44 84 45 00 Concerts 90–200F. www.cite-musique.fr*
An oval-shaped auditorium seating 800-1,200. Weekend concerts tend to be organized around a particular theme. Jazz classical, contemporary and traditional music concerts. There is also a multi-media library and information center on music and dance (Tue-Sun until 6pm).

Le Trabendo (G D2)
→ *211, ave Jean-Jaurès (20th) Tel. 01 42 54 07 47 for program information.*
Formerly known as Hot Brass, this auditorium seats 700 and is filled with the graffiti art of Futura 2000. Modern venue for rock, world music and jazz concerts. Entrance 80–120F.

SHOPPING

Marché de Belleville (G B5-C6)

→ *Mº Belleville and Ménilmontant*
Every Tuesday and Friday the central divider strip of the Boulevard de Belleville plays host to one of the largest markets in Paris. Hundreds of colorful stalls selling fruit, vegetables, spices ... the crowds are extraordinary.

Épicerie Le Caire (G C5)
→ *63, rue de Belleville (19th) Tel. 01 42 06 06 01 Tue–Sun 10am–10pm.*
Adel Moussa's grocery store resembles a *souk*: olives, spices, cheese, rice, semolina and Egyptian specialties (cardamom-flavored coffee, *mammoul* with dates, pistachio or walnuts *borek* with cheese or spinach ...).

Nani (G D5)
→ *104, rue de Belleville (20th) Tel. 01 47 97 38 05 Sun–Fri 8am–7.30pm.*
Since 1962 Nani has made the locals salivate. The store's narrow front hides a small, long pâtisserie. On the left are classics like lemon tarts, strawberry gâteaux, *millefeuille* pastries... on the right, a mountain of oriental pastries: *makroud, baklava, oreillettes* with honey...).

The immense Bibliothèque Nationale (1997) is seen as a symbol for the east side of Paris, an area which has totally changed over the past two decades. The industrial wastelands of Bercy and Austerlitz have provided architects and town planners with invaluable experimental freedom, resulting in the Institut du Monde Arabe in 1987, the Ministère des Finances in 1989, the Parc de Bercy in 1994 and various new residential districts. Below the Jardin des Plantes the boulevards lead to the Place d'Italie and, toward the Porte de Choisy, to the towers of Chinatown (1970), erected at the foot of the Butte-aux-Cailles.

ZIRYAB

LE TRAIN BLEU

RESTAURANTS

Le Temps des Cerises (H A4)
→ 18, rue de la Butte-aux-Cailles (13*th*)
Tel. 01 45 89 69 48
Mon-Sat noon–2pm, 7.30–11.45pm.
Workers' cooperative offering an informal place to eat. Home-cooking with the occasional exotic influence. Generous portions, set 3-course menu at 78F. If it's full, try the nearby *Chez Gladines* (Basque specialties) or *Chez Paul* (a little more expensive).

Phô Ban Cuon 14 (H B4)
→ 129, ave. de Choisy (13*th*)
Tel. 01 45 83 61 15
Daily 9am–11pm.
On the borders of Chinatown, this is the hangout for *phô* enthusiasts (it is available all day). The Vietnamese noodle soup served here is amongst the best in Paris. Around 70F.

Le Ziryab (H B1)
→ *Institut du Monde Arabe 1, rue des Fossés-St-Bernard (5*th*). Tel. 01 53 10 10 17
Tue-Sun
noon–3pm (restaurant), 3.30-6pm (tearoom).
At the top of the Institut du Monde Arabe, there is a bird's-eye view of Notre

Dame, north to the Bastille and beyond: a magnificent setting in which to savour a quail *pastilla* (110F), a lamb tajine (140F) or maybe just a mint tea made with fresh leaves (20F).

Le Petit Marguery (H A3)
→ 9, bd de Port-Royal (13*th*)
Tel. 01 43 31 58 59 Tue-Sat
noon–2pm, 7.30–10.15pm.
The epitome of the French bistro, run by the adorable Cousin brothers. Bourgeois cuisine and game in season. Generous portions and regional wine. Tradition at its best. Set menu 165F.

Etchegorry (H A4)
→ 41–43, rue Croulebarbe (13*th*) Tel. 01 44 08 83 51
Mon-Sat noon–2.30pm, 7–10.30pm.
South-west French cuisine, especially influenced by the Basque country. Reasonable prices. Set menu 145F, gastronomic menu (with *foie gras*) 180F.

Le Train Bleu (H D1)
→ *Gare de Lyon 20, bd Diderot (12*th*)
Tel. 01 43 43 09 06
Daily 11.30am–3pm, 7–11pm
One of a kind: a station restaurant in a listed historic building. Extraordinary décor with

LIE EN TÊTE   BERCY VILLAGE   LES ABEILLES

frescos depicting the stops along the Paris-Lyon-Méditerranée (PLM) line, statues, moldings and 1900s furniture. Eager service and good classic cuisine: creamed lentils with bacon and browned croûtons, pike dumplings with crawfish. Set menu 255F.

CAFÉS, TEAROOMS

Bercy Village (H F4)
→ *Cour St-Émilion (12ʰ)*
These former Bercy *chais* (wine cellars) are the perfect place to stop for a drink as they have now been refurbished and turned into café-restaurants.

Salon de Thé de la Mosquée de Paris (H A2)
→ *39, rue Geoffroy-St-Hilaire (5ʰ)*
Tel. 01 43 31 18 14 Daily 8am–11.30pm (tearoom)
Tel. 01 43 31 18 14 (baths)
Women: Mon, Wed-Sat 10am–9pm (Fri 2–9pm)
Men: Tue 2–9pm;
Sun 10am–9pm.
Small tables under the olive and fig trees, the murmur of the fountain, the sweet smell of incense: this setting is straight out of *The Arabian Nights*: Moorish interior and sofas inside

the mosque. Eat a full meal or simply sample the crunchy honey-, almond-, or orange flower-flavored pastries. But before that, why not indulge yourself in the hammam's tempting steam rooms?

BARS, CINEMA, MUSIC VENUES

La Folie en tête (H A4)
→ *33, rue de la Butte-aux-Cailles (13ʰ)*
Tel. 01 45 80 65 99
Mon–Sat 5pm–2am.
A lively little café decorated with wooden musical instruments from all over the world, in the heart of the old village of Butte-aux-Cailles. Contemporary art exhibitions, occasional concerts, storytelling and theater.

Batofar (H E3)
→ *Port de la Gare, opposite 11, quai Mauriac (13ʰ) Tel. 01 56 29 10 00 (times vary depending on the program).*
The latest addition to the trendy fleet of restaurants anchored at the foot of the Bibliothèque Nationale. Steel hull and interior: urban films and exhibitions, electronic music and international

DJs – and a crowd on hand to rock the boat!

Guinguette Pirate (H E3)
→ *Port de la Gare, facing n° 11, quai Mauriac (13ʰ) Tel. 01 56 29 10 20 Daily from 7pm.*
Eclectic clientele and a charged atmosphere in this wooden junk built in Saigon in 1970. Its neighbor, the barge *Makara*, has a different program of music every evening: rock, world music, dub, jazz, reggae, funk, trip hop. Shows for children.

Gaumont Grand Écran Italie (H A4)
→ *30, pl. d'Italie (13ʰ)*
Tel. 01 45 80 86 78
Spectacular films shown on the biggest screen in Paris (860 sq ft). Housed in a monochrome, aluminium building designed by Kenzo Tange.

SHOPPING

Galeries d'Art de la rue Louise-Weiss (H C3-C4)
These art galleries now occupy the workshops which once flourished in this former industrial district. They continue the tradition of the great 'Frigos', the former refrigerated warehouses

of Bercy converted into studios which have, since 1980, welcomed into their thousands of square feet at n° 91, quai Panhard-et-Levassor, a plethora of painters, sculptors, architects and musicians.

Les Abeilles (H A4)
→ *21, rue de la Butte-aux-Cailles (13ʰ)*
Tel. 01 45 81 43 48
Tue-Sat 11am–7pm.
Fifty types of honey from all over France.

Mavrommatis (H A2)
→ *47, rue Censier (5ʰ)*
Tel. 01 45 35 96 50
Daily 9am–10pm.
A lovely top-of-the-range Greek deli selling various *meze: talassini*, stuffed vine leaves, aubergine or pepper *caviar* (puréed with a garlic and olive oil marinade). Wide choice of Greek and Cypriot wines.

Marché de la Place Monge (H A2)
→ *Wed, Fri and Sun.*
Attractive little food market close to the Rue Mouffetard.

Tang Frères (H B2)
→ *48, ave. d'Ivry (13ʰ)*
Tel. 01 45 70 80 00
Tue-Sun 9am–7.30pm.
The largest and most famous Asian super-market in the capital, a few steps from Place d'Italie (off the map).

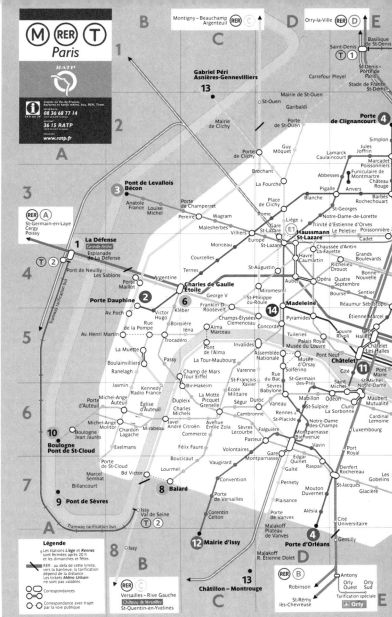

Letters (**A, B, C...**) relate to the matching sections. Letters on their own refer to the useful addresses spreads and, where followed by a star (**A★**), to the places of interest on the fold-out map of the area.